Margie in the Morning

Margie in the Morning

Robbie Saltaire

coolgrovepress

First published in the United States by
Coolgrove Press, an imprint of
Cool Grove Publishing, Inc. New York.
512 Argyle Road, Brooklyn, NY 11218

For permissions and other inquiries
write to info@coolgrove.com

ISBN 13: 978-1-887276-97-9
Library of Congress Control Number: 2022933399

Cover art: Jorge Lopez

Cool Grove Press is a past recipient of
Community of Literary Magazines and Presses [CLMP]'s
Face Out Re-grant for marketing

This book is distributed to the trade by Ingram Spark

Media alchemy by Kiku

coolgrovepress

*To my parents
with boundless gratitude*

Margie in the Morning

For the Methode of a Poet historical is not such, as of an Historiographer.   For an Historiographer discourseth of affayres orderly as they were done, but a poet thrusteth into the middle, where it most concerneth him, and there recoursing to the things gone past, and divining of things to come, maketh a pleasing analysis of all.

— Edmund Spenser

Experience shows that a strong memory is commonly coupled with a weak judgment.

— Michel de Montaigne

Many years from now when I'm so old and crapped up that I need an occasional aide to help me on my daily path, I would like her to be an attractive New Yorker with an accent so heavy that my name, Robert, sounds like a nasal "Rabbit" from her bright lipstick mouth. I will permit her to smoke though my doctors don't advise it, and drift on the music of her New York womanhood among the memories that her voice evokes as it soars above the high-rise view of a neighborhood where I've never lived before—a nice part of Queens where you can sometimes smell the water or even some new vista of my native Manhattan. My family doesn't figure in this occasional fantasy, just the appealing figure of a good-looking woman thirty or forty years younger than I with a voice from my childhood streets. Lately she's short, dark-haired and Italian, sometimes taller and bleached blonde, always seen against the background of the city I return to at the end of my years, bringing me joy with stories of her life in the tingling accent of the antique New York tongue.

One day last August—or was it the one before?—I was sitting at my desk with exactly such a view over midtown south-west, waiting to be fired and feeling reasonably young, just returned to my office after a meeting on the 99th floor of the South Tower. I'd been helping a friend with a proposal to a client who was nice enough to see her but barely able to stay in the room for the eight minutes it took to make the pitch. We all sat uncomfortably as the building swayed in a strong summer wind that made me feel a little queasy, a perfect special effect for the hopeless meeting.

I'd been glad to get back to my company's big, lovely and almost empty office. We'd gone from 95 employees in December to 40 in April and with Labor Day around the corner we were down to an even dozen. I sat back in my $600 chair with no billable work to occupy my mind and the proverbial rest of my life close at hand, and I wondered—how much time is left for me to eat bread and drink wine on this lovely earth after my employer releases me into an impossible job market? So I fired up my browser, did a quick search for a life expectancy calculator and found one at *YourLongLife.com* which promised an accurate estimate of my remaining moments under the warming sun and the silvery moon, whose glow once lit the brightest part of my life.

The calculator was a busy screen with many small boxes to hold the numeric markers of my existence. Hopefully I typed in the numbers of my sins and diseases, drinks and smokes, fatty meats, inches and pounds and moving violations, heart attacks of parents and grandparents with ancestral cancers fatal and otherwise—and quickly discovered that I had 1,324,511,999 seconds of sublunary joy before departing for regions lit by stars yet unknown, at precisely 3:18PM on Thursday, February 6, 2042. But no! make that 1,324,511,998 seconds to live! then 1,324,511,997… 1,324,511,996…1,324,511,995 and tick tick tock in a little pop-up box to the last digit of my estimated time. Amused, I called the website across the room to Suzanne, the lovely and hilarious ex-Morgan Stanley vice president and to the gifted young Steve, astrophysicist and DJ. They quickly cast their fates to the web and we laughed together to see our departures all scheduled between 3 and 6PM, though on widely varying years. Was this post-prandial coincidence merely a too-simple algorithm or the statistically significant effect of food on aged guts? I left the question to the beautiful Wall Street computer scientist and the carrot-topped master of Jovian gravitation and returned to the solitary exploration of my own 1,324,511,350 seconds.

The first thing I did was close the ticking calculator with its false exactitude and authentic reek of mortality. Having already consulted that morning the New York Times, Washington Post, LA Times, Boston Globe, Times of London, the Guardian, Atlantic, Time, Newsweek, Salon, New Republic, Roll Call, Variety, Publishers Weekly and the Florida State Department of

Corrections—a fine web site, one of the best!—I decided to explore *YourLongLife.com* a little more because tucked away on the lower left of the home page was a hyperlink with the incredible promise that like more heroic and better narrators before me, I could Search the Social Security Death File to Find Any Death.

Lacking the faith of my glorious predecessors, I disbelieved that I could actually Find Any Death so I said aloud but softly, in close imitation of my grandfather's heavily Yiddish accent—'America, deh tings dey got heah, oy!' and gave my face a little Jack Benny slap. Then I typed his name, Morris Kazan, into the First Name / Last Name fields and pressed ENTER, and three seconds later I saw a page listing the six Morris Kazans who had died with Social Security cards and there he was at the top: my own grandfather known as Pop, born under Czar Nicholas I in Bialystok, Poland on December 2, 1886 and died under Gerry Ford on August 8, 1976 in the Bronx, New York. And his Social Security number— 428-56-9812 if you want one graced with an abundance of good fortune, most of it self-made, that lasted 90 years until he died with sound mind and few regrets other than his eldest daughter's marriage to a sociopathic violin repairman.

Amazed to find my beloved grandparent in less time than it takes to look up a phone number, I typed in the name of Joan Milton, my best friend's mother and a dear friend to me who died suddenly at a vigorous and wealthy 67 of a three-day viral pneumonia in Palm Springs. Bing! Born April 11—my mother's birthday too—and died on February 11, 1991. Both before and after her estate passed through the hands of Uncle Sam you could have used 228-39-0467 to access more than enough money to satisfy any of your reasonable and quite a few unreasonable needs without the necessity of actually working for a living. Having myself managed a financial planning call center where we allocated millions of dollars a day based on spoken SSNs along with information easily found in the phone book, I was surprised to find this lode of personal info available for the price of a mouse click. So I typed in the big one, that most faithful dreamer and creator, deeply adored and still missed every day after six years: my father—and instantly I see the name I love with that wonderful date, May 9, when he came into this place he enjoyed so much, and the other date which I don't love but do respect for its power and mystery, October 6 when after a gratefully short illness he left the inhabitants of this world to whom he'd brought so much happiness and good. Hi dad! I always smile when I think of him and I was smiling then as I'm smiling now.

My beautiful aunt Belle who doted over me, swept away at the awful, ugly age of 49: yes, she died on Christmas eve 1971 as I remember and her SSN was

387-71-9892 which of course I never knew. My mother's best friend Lucy whose two husbands committed suicide thirty years apart, followed by her twenty-five years later at the reasonable age of 88 on Halloween: darling Lucille, how wonderful to see your name, and it was very kind of you not to tell my mother of your plans. I knew you were a member of the Hemlock Society and a firm believer in arranging your own departure even if your mode of thought was supremely un-Socratic—epicurean, Ecclesiastean, existentialist even—but I never knew the SSN you left behind, 023-44-5551.

****

A reasonable reader might at this point believe me unreasonably interested in death and think that I, like a more talented and better-known narrator, often find life a drab and drear November in my soul, and join processions that follow behind coffins. Such is not the case: I smile at babies and they smile back; take huge delight in the society of cardinals—the brightly-colored gentle ones that sing sweetly in the air and cherish their young in safely-hidden nests, that is; fill with joy at the sight of a Tiepolo on the wall, a Twain on the page or a Hepburn on the screen, Audrey preferred but Katherine often amuses; and find daily unsarcastic joys in the parade of breathing mortals, friends and passing strangers both. Alone, I spend happy hours with a stupid grin lying in thick clover looking at white clouds moving south and east across the sky, listening to the sound of the wind and the birds in the trees of my natal lawn on the edge of the woods; and when finances and time permit I float happily in a quiet portion of the one great sea, lying on my back as I do in my native clover, supported more softly though not so well by the warm tides of Cape Cod's perfect shallow.

In fact, by 6:30 most mornings I find myself glad to be alive in the present and optimistic about the future despite the fact that I don't have a job and after a year out of work I'm utterly broke and financially dependent on my wife, who has only recently emerged from a phase when she was not at all pleased to be married to me. But still I remain well disposed. Ask Peleg—what a fine name to see on a young man's nametag!—who sold me a wah-wah pedal at the music store after my first session at the Department of Labor, a/k/a the unemployment office, which was called to a short stop on that morning of September 11 when the cell phones began to go off in the conference room and I knew that I'd be at liberty longer than I planned: ask that handsome red-haired salesman or my friends or my son, my mother or my innumerable coworkers in the various cash-heaps of humanity where I have toiled, and sometimes merely passed the time, over the past twenty years. You may even ask my wife and she will probably agree: I love life, I enjoy most of the people in it without condescension (after having been mightily humbled a few years ago) and I usually have fun just walking along the street.

All these happy facts, however, don't change the reality that many of my favorite people are dead. And so that day last August when I returned from the 99th floor of the South Tower and browsed on *YourLongLife.com* while waiting to be fired, and I didn't have long to wait since that day was August 21 and my last day on the payroll would be August 24, I entered the name of the closest of my ex-girlfriends whom I knew to be dead, the lovely Jennifer Cohen—and found nothing, not surprising because poor Jennifer proudly took her husband's name just a year before her galloping rare cancer appeared, and since I didn't know anything about that unhappy man except his dreadful heartbreak I would never know Jen's SSN. Then I looked for another girlfriend who no longer played in our green mortal meadows—more accurately, my childhood friend and occasional adult sex partner Marjorie Hollister, the slim, pretty, reddish brunette I met in 4th grade when we discovered that we both liked chewing the raw macaroni in Mrs. Haupt's art class. I had seen Margie over the years into our mid-twenties when she wanted sex, which was always accompanied by a reminiscent flavor of the childhood friendship we'd shared as nine-year olds, though in our adulthood—or what passed for it at the time—we rarely socialized since she considered me too bohemian while she, Jewish as I was, had a Katherine Hepburn accent and aspired to the manner of old New York as in the nine-room east 72nd street apartment where she grew up. Poor Margie ended her own life when no treatment could alleviate her deep elemental sadness which I'd never grasped in my good-natured youthful ignorance as her on-call sex pony; so I typed the appropriate elements of her identity into the First Name / Last Name fields of the great American Death File and banged the convenient ENTER key.

And here she is! Hello sweet, sad Margie, born August 28, 195x and died October 23, 197x, SSN 064-27-9831. Place of birth: New York, New York; last known residence: New York, New York, where I saw her fine and tightly drawn face for the last time on a summer evening in Central Park where we sometimes had sex on deserted lawns near Fifth Avenue as we did on benches in the various parks and three-bench porches overlooking the East River, though I had officially "devirginated" her lovely writhing tan body—a word she liked—at 4AM on a late spring morning on my bed in the room where I grew up, while my father slept down the hall. That was the first time we ever took our pleasure indoors, and one of the very few.

The last time I saw Margie in this beautiful, confusing world, we walked around Central Park on a summer evening when the paths were full, holding hands like the old friends we were. The spark for sex wasn't there for her so we just chatted pleasantly. (It wasn't there for me either but would have returned in about two seconds at the slightest opportunity.) The last time I heard her, though—or imagined I did—was something else again, on a bus going down Fifth Avenue on a sunny morning in late March, four years after she died. I was on my way to work at my first job as a paralegal at one of the great American law firms, also now deceased, called Donovan Leisure Newton & Irvine where for $13,200 a year I had my own office on the 41st floor of the RCA building looking north across Manhattan, four weeks a year vacation and every imaginable holiday plus twelve sick days I religiously observed with hangovers if not flu, along with frequent first class, all-you-can-drink travel to and from southern California on behalf of an idiotic client who had paid out a billion dollars in a lawsuit— actually paid $998 million in 1978 dollars!—and was suing the international uranium cartel for treble damages under anti-trust law, a fat $3 billion, which is where Donovan Leisure and I came in. Much about this was very pleasant and I managed to save a thousand dollars a year, mainly the overtime I was paid on top of my salary.

The night before that warm day when I last heard Margie—or thought I did—was a cold remembrance of winter, which had been banished by the calendar but not yet by nature. I left the firm promptly at 5:30, took the Madison Avenue bus home, stopped off at my corner pub for a few beers and a hamburger and then walked down Fifth to climb the high, wide steps of the Metropolitan Museum of Art for the opening of a new show called Treasures of the Kremlin. My parents were small-time donors and often gave me their invitations to these receptions; sometimes the art was wonderful and sometimes just OK but there were always crowds of fashionable women in bright clothes and brighter jewelry sipping cocktails amidst the glories of the past, and seeking new pleasures in the present. This evening, after stopping at the lobby bar for two large and icy vodkas from one of the Cuban bartenders whom I befriended during the delicious long afternoons of my post-collegiate years as tutor, researcher and would-be writer, I headed up alone to the uncrowded galleries.

As I remember them, these treasures of the Kremlin were mainly enormous silver tea kettles, vases and table sculptures inlaid with a black enamel-like coating called niello, nothing to scoff at but more curiosity to my eyes than glory and the reason why the galleries were virtually empty. After a moment in the first dim room I became aware of an attractive young woman who looked, if you'll pardon the expression, intensely American. She wore a long, straight, antique dress of sky blue silk down to her ankles, gold wire glasses around her bright green eyes and straight dirty blonde hair pulled back from a clean, pretty, somewhat flat face that showed a genuine smile. I forget what she said as I moved through the doorway into the next room, but I found her walking alongside me as we chatted and I enjoyed her friendliness and fresh-scrubbed American womanhood, so unlike the glitzy honey-pots young and old roiling the lobby. We chatted, she sparkled and at some point in the second room she touched my shoulder and I thought, "This may become a very pleasant evening." In the third room she was right with me, her hand at the middle of my back and in the fourth room, still chatting happily about the art, she had her arm around my waist.

As we left the exhibit holding hands down the staircase into the great main hall I was relaxed and hopeful, looking forward to a pleasurable evening getting to know her and her pale, slim body and her interesting smile. What a pleasant change to have a woman making all the moves! And such an unusual one, a very pretty cross between the 1960's and the 1890's, hippie Vermont and antique Pennsylvania. So back to the lobby, back to the bar, back to the iced vodka from my Cuban amigo and then to a small table in the huge room bright with flowers and the sounds of a string quartet. The looks of the women who hadn't found a man seemed to make my new friend smile even brighter; she held my hand in both of hers and told me how much she liked me and wanted to have a relationship.

"I like you too, Linda, very much," I said as her green eyes glistened like a thick lawn just watered in the late morning sun. And I did like her—she seemed nice, she was intelligent, attractive and I was ready for whatever might come however long it lasted, as long as it started this night.

"But I'm sorry, Robbie, it's going to have to be a platonic relationship."

I squinted a bit, pretending a concern I didn't feel because three women had previously used the p-word to me and all three invited me to share their bed the same night that they used the philosophical phrase. Many other women have preferred me at arm's length but none of them invoked Socrates' most famous student.

"I'm sorry to hear that, Linda, I'm really attracted to you, why do think we need to have to a platonic relationship?"

"I have a lover, here in New York." There was a new, serious tone to her voice and the light in her green eyes dimmed for a moment. But at that point in my life the only lovers of potential sex partners who inhibited me were those in the same room at the same time—and not always then—so I just held our hands together on the table and nodded in actual sympathy.

She nodded back at me and then said,

"My lover is John Lennon," and her eyes became all bright again as she thought of him and a pretty smile returned to her thin, barely glossed lips.

I don't recall thinking much of anything and I felt just as relaxed as I'd been before, but I was proud of myself as I heard my voice say in a kind, calm tone, "Do you know him?"

The answer alas was no, and so we went home to her apartment across the street from The Dakota on 72nd street where John and Yoko lived. It was decorated with rare photographs of Lennon and the Beatles; a few shots of the stocky, muscular, short-haired woman she'd lived with for five years; and a picture of the fiancé she'd broken up with recently: because she loved John and was "saving" herself for him, she had never actually had sexual intercourse with this fiancé, or her other two former fiancés, or with any other man. Nor had she ever met John Lennon. And when I asked why she didn't just say hello to him on the street, she was horrified and told me, "No, that would be just like a groupie!"

Her plan was more complex: to write a brilliant novel, meet John at one of those New York cocktail parties where she as a successful and lovely young novelist would eventually encounter him, then use her wit, intelligence and beauty to steal him away from Yoko. (Yoko had been good for him once but her time had passed and now it was Linda who could bring him happiness.) And her idea for the novel was a good one, too: a gay Native American and a straight Anglo become best friends in combat in Vietnam, briefly lovers under fire, then go their separate ways when they leave the Army, but events bring them back together and the straight one struggles with his deep feelings for his friend.

Once I saw the picture of her husky room-mate, heard her confess her 28-year-old virginity and learned the plot of her would-be novel, I could understand how the obsession with Lennon provided her with an effective if literally crazy way to avoid practicing heterosexuality. Still, we ate rum-raisin ice cream with Jack Daniels, a childhood sweet-shoppe of a high, and we kissed and she cried and I took her number, and she said that guys always said they'd call but never did. I said I would and eventually I did, once to be polite. Later when John Lennon was murdered I thought she'd either be much better or much worse, and two years after that at another opening at the Met I saw her looking not at all older, still fresh-scrubbed Americana in another antique dress, this one pale pink, with the same knowing smile on her thin lips, green eyes twinkling just as brightly.

I left her apartment at 11:30 and decided to walk home through Central Park because I love the park in the snow. It was a cold March night after a warm and sunny day though the previous night we'd had six inches of snow, not an unusual sequence of weather for New York City any time between December and March. I entered the park at 72nd street just across the avenue from John and Yoko's high-ceilinged residence and with the dimmed skyline of Central Park West behind me and the few lights of Fifth Avenue a soft horizon ahead, I walked into the lamp-lit darkness past the snowy patch that would soon be known as Strawberry Fields, in memento moria of my new friend's imaginary lover.

Tip-toeing across the melted snow that was hardened to a midnight's slick, quick-stepping the long way home through the bare trees, carrying only the feelings I needed for this journey through cool air and dark-etched landscape, I skirted the southern edge of the rowboat lake where I'd seen a fifty-pound snapping turtle lumbering weirdly one summer morning, and I found myself walking east into an open space across the crusty snow of a meadow that was brightened from its rim by antique iron streetlamps. I recognized this lawn, facing east on a low ridge over the pond, as the place where I'd happily played the dying game with my schoolmates. Somehow I recall fourth grade as the dying game's big year—which means Margie might have played it with me because I met her when I was skipped into fourth—

and one teacher made it popular, I don't remember his name, but we'd gather on the lawn where he'd pretend to have a machine gun and call us out one by one.

We children of uncountable westerns and cannon-flashing war movies would be standing alongside one of those gray granite mini-mountains of Manhattan bedrock, so excited and happy as he called us each by name to run at him across the grass, and he'd rat-tat-tat imaginary bullets as fast as he could spit them out. Was he a veteran of World War II or Korea indulging some bizarre fantasy or merely having fun with us, such great fun that we adored? I'll never know but our thrill was to die dramatically, sprawling and tumbling, lurching and twitching like the onscreen heroes and bad guys we'd seen stumble into eternity a thousand times before. I always felt the most intense, happy excitement just before running into the clattering imaginary weapon, racing to my acrobatic doom among friends already sprawled across the meadow, my face filled with an effervescent twinkly anticipation of the heart not unlike later dances and early dates, feeling that all eyes were on me, should be on me, must be on me—throwing myself through the air, landing with soulful and powerful twitches, caressing the grass and dark dirt as I finally came to rest.

At first the girls just watched the boys play our historical role as cannon fodder but then a few of them demanded to play and they had great fun dying just as gloriously as we did, and soon both sexes looked forward to the dying game as the great pleasure of recess; but after a month of eerie coed glee our joy was banned—some parents of the girls complained because when daring daughters died well, their skirts immodestly blossomed as they tumbled to the all-embracing earth. And the dying game was no more.

The paths of Central Park, the edges of its lawns and meadows, are lit quite well at night and by the lights of the glowing lamps all around and the rising moon to the east over Fifth, I made a good pace crunching through the snow of that happy meadow of imaginary doom with its doubly-ethereal .50 calibers and ghostly childish corduroy dresses kicked up high by happy feet. Passing across the meadow's border that was a dark stand of shadows under a tall regiment of trees I emerged onto great acres of asphalt, the concert grounds surrounding Central Park's Bandshell. It was there as a 17-year old loaded to the gills on LSD—the fabled crypto-chemist Owsley's first acid answer to the popular Orange Sunshine—that I found myself getting way too high under a hot July sun as I listened to the Grateful Dead, and I forced myself home to avoid the powerful imminence of a trip I didn't think I could handle. And later that afternoon after a long bath I sat in the living room with my angry mother and first discovered her as a person and not merely as a mom, and if it was a revelation in her anger instead of her life-defining love and acceptance, it was enlightening nonetheless.

This cool night a decade later I walked carefully around the ice that was scattered on the wide asphalt esplanade between the towering elms where I'd bicycled as a child, across the squared football-field of benches facing the Bandshell in the snow-spattered night, and climbed up the short steps to the empty stage of the huge concrete semi-sphere. I retreated to the back of its shadowy arc, looked out across the stage towards the dim landscape of the park and I launched my voice into a booming doo-wop rhythm to replicate the notes that my brother first sounded in the tiled shower of our fraternal bathroom— "Each night before I go to bed, bend my knees and bow my head, pray to the angels up above, send me down someone to love! Botta botta boom tee-ay tee-ay, botta botta boom tee-ay. Botta botta boom tee-ay tee-ay, botta botta boom tee-ay...." But despite the heartfelt resonance in my body and my earnest effort to share it with the world, the vast and perfect Bandshell wouldn't echo the rolling sound I heard in my head.

I suddenly felt just a little bit tired, so I slowly walked flat-footed to the edge of the stage and gazed at the black and white mysterious beauty of the park laid out for my eyes only and—I paused. Briefly. In a moment of quiet I found my breath, felt the park and the night pleasantly sharp in my cold temples and decided to head home. I carefully climbed down from the stage and ascended the icy steps behind the Bandshell leading up to a dense grove of tall bushes planted a hundred years ago to shelter city folk from the summer sun—and later, Dustin Hoffman in Kramer vs. Kramer when he told his sad son that Meryl Streep had won him at the custody hearing. The planting was mainly ancient mountain laurel twined thick with younger vines bare-branched through a rustic framework of gnarled posts and beams. Its ivy ceiling, now dead straw, wove through a wire woof to cool this shady aisle against the elemental New York August, though with all the leaves down it was brighter than you'd think in the March midnight with a three-quarters moon in the east. My eyes reflexively spotted the way dark and light under the shadow-streaked moon between dry asphalt and the slick, and I came out of the old grove to find myself facing a black iron fence with an open gate that led to a bright and treeless world. It was a familiar sight indeed and so very welcoming, the playground at 72nd street where I played each day at recess from first grade through fifth!

Though man-made asphalt, concrete and steel, the playground charmed my eyes and the rest of me and I felt only the confident, happy motion of my body forward through the cool night under the moon with my face in full smile. The wide place wrapped itself all around me as I walked past the swings where we swung and told stories and lies, past the seesaws where we bounced and jumped and flung each other at the sky, past the low fences that were more fun to climb than the jungle gym; and past the open patch where we fifth-grade boys declared ourselves the F-100's, a well-planned secret society that we sprung in first strike surprise at our girlish enemies, zooming at them with arms outstretched, threatening and howling aggressive circles around our shrieking victims.

(A workable peace between the sexes returned in sixth grade when Mrs. McNeil, a beautifully-dressed, Vanderbilt-schooled but violently immature southern debutante, tried to rule us with pinches, twisted ears and threatening marks in her little black book, even rougher on the girls than on the boys. We children of upper-middle class Manhattan had never been struck by a teacher in our lives, so we united in rebellion against her just as our changing bodies were bringing us closer together. First we drove her crying from the classroom one day by shooting doubled-up paper clips from quadruple rubber-band launchers in a carefully planned and relentless assault against the big, floppy sheet of poster paper where she was diagramming outline structures I. II. and III. With boys and girls both literally shredding the paper with an insistent a-rhythmic slapping attack of tiny steel missiles, making the top sheet and then the papers below hop and twitch in the fury of our fire, she stomped and pouted and screamed but we refused to stop as our paper-clip terror sliced pieces off the top sheet flapping onto the floor—really and truly. When she ran furious out the door we laughed and cheered; she returned with surprising calm in a few minutes and her peace lasted for several weeks until she gradually returned to her old ways though with less visible anger behind her piercing long fingernails and twisted earlobes.)

(Her reign of terror ended one day during twenty minutes of free play among the trees and paths of Central Park when we found two surly teenage boys willing to take six dollars to steal the black leather notebook that she kept in her gleaming patent-leather pocketbook to record our alleged misdeeds. After the payoff we saw no action for a few minutes and we thought the boys had fooled us like so many hustlers before and since—after all, you can't cheat an honest man—but to our fearful delight they swooped back to grab the pocketbook and disappeared through a windbreak of tall maples screened by younger pines. Mrs. McNeil was more angry than frightened, a typical reaction to petty crime and ten minutes later when we found the pocketbook under a bush all was recovered except for the black book: wallet and money were there but not her archive of sixth-grade sin. It seemed to us that she realized what happened but she wisely said nothing and neither did we, except for a few fake expressions of regret and relief. But the point had finally been made with enough authority to penetrate even her violent determination and thereafter she kept her hands and her threats to herself and focused on the actual teaching, at which she excelled.)

So past that asphalt flat where the girl-hating F-100's had launched their first strike and out the eastern gate of the playground into the dark, tree-shaded entrance, the gate we entered each day from Fifth Avenue past the big stone statue of Mother Goose, witch-like in a tall hat riding a great bird. This was the gate we raced to every day in the impossibly light strides of playful children and up until the middle of third grade when I was skipped into fourth I alternated first place through those daily races with long-legged Art Pfeiffer, born as I was April 18 in the year of their lord 195x. Art's father was a surgeon and his mother a former Miss Egypt who met her husband selling him aftershave on the floor of Bloomingdales; like many a surgeon before and since, Art's dad felt himself closer to divine than human law so when eight-year old Art visited my family's summer home he carried a doctor's black bag filled with a thousand and one different pills, real pills, and it was only my older brother's quick intervention that kept me from downing the mixed mash we'd made of them. And later, though the girls in second grade were horrified when Art brought a huge glass jar to show-and-tell with a deer's bloody foreleg inside, like most of the boys I thought it was kind of cool, though I was repulsed when we were driving with his father on a dirt road in northern Westchester and his dad spotted a small groundhog in a ditch: he stopped the car, took a shotgun out of the trunk and gave it to eight-year Art who turned the once-furry thing into a nasty puree.

I left Art permanently behind when I was skipped from third grade into fourth near enough Lincoln's birthday that memorizing the Gettysburg address was the first major task I remember. Yet even in fourth I was often the fastest boy through the gate running neck and neck with Michael Nealon, whose mother earned a living sketching the luxuriously long-limbed lingerie models who brightened the New York Times with glowing black and white beauty. Michael's living room was the studio where his mother drew the female forms that so embarrassed him—and to this day he finds no delight in those smooth curves where I find life itself—but the rest of us ten- and eleven-year boys treasured those brief walks through the foyer to his room and judging by their smiles, the models were amused too.

This moonlit night I walked the other way briskly out that gate where once I'd run on the flying feet of a happy boy, faster than which there is no joy, now enjoying my man's strong body moving across this well-paved portion of the still-lovely earth, just inside the park from Fifth, the risen moon sparkling the snow on small patches of grass around the curved intersection where 72nd street joins the Park Drive and loops west past Bethesda Fountain. No cars, no sounds but a faint wind through the stripped branches and my own breath and wintry steps, the just-frozen air pleasantly chilled in my nose and throat. I descended the small hill to the drained and frozen Model Boat Pond, not on the stairs that were slick with ice but half-running, half-hopping from heel to heel down the hill trusting to my balance, alone and happy in the cool night as I zagged towards the almost empty concrete oval eighty yards long, spattered with snow and leaves and ringed with a great shining nimbus from the old-fashioned wrought iron streetlamps around it.

The heel-hop is a good technique on snow that's crusted on top but not always thick enough to support you, with every step your crunching heels penetrate the slippery stuff to the firmness below then you launch up again, and I made it easily to the drained Boat Pond where the black iron lamps with their so-bright lights welcomed me into their furiously glowing dream. Radiating more than visual energy into the cool night air, the lamps seemed anxious in their solitude, uneasily bereft of the model sail-boaters, dog-walkers, childcare providers and singles in search of greater numbers who crowd the space through four seasons of daylight. Bereft in fact of all visitors but me and presumably a few crayfish slumbering under the leaves and branches that gloomed under scant inches of pooled water and snow.

My descent had been noisy and left me panting happily at the southwest curve of the long concrete Pond with eyes startled by the intensity of its lamps and the shimmering, unnatural glow of their curving lines of luminescence against the dark wall of Fifth, and their patchy white bursts of reflection in the unevenly frozen water. Though I wished to walk north as quickly as possible, the paving stone perimeter of the Boat Pond was too slick with ice from the day's snow melt—the high had risen to 49 and sunny, streams of liberated water had naturally emerged from yesternight's snow and taken the gravity-fueled path of least resistance down every slope to the nearest surface of the great valley which happily received them into the quick frost of evening. So I walked in the crunchy snow alongside the iced pavement, the safest way for me to travel back to my own neighborhood and I found myself edging along a tiny lawn where many years ago in an early example of my intimations of omnipotence I had tossed a rock high into the air to impress the second-grade girl I had a play-date with. It was before I was skipped and I don't remember her name but I do remember her worshipful attention and the immense Fifth Avenue apartment where she lived in fourteen rooms with long, long hallways that crackled with static electricity. There in the park on a fall afternoon in those happy days when the World Series knew only daylight, I tossed a rock high into the air and far away as she squealed from a safe distance in fear and utter delight. I did it again and strolled calmly towards her feeling that self-confidence which has so often marked my most memorable self-inflicted pains—and in that I'm no different from most two-legged animals of whom I'm aware.

I looked up at the blue sky with what I remember even now as a self-satisfied, happy smile and I must have thrown the rock really high because I had time to take a few steps, soak in the girl's babyish love and look confidently up before the rock smacked straight into my skull, knocking me to my knees in surprise and sending my own small stream of warm liquid towards the ever-welcoming earth. I remember the terrible shock on the face of the uniformed maid who had brought us to the park, which now I understand even better because she was worried about her job as well as my head. But she quickly walked us to the girl's pediatrician nearby, right off Fifth, and all ended happily because my skull, like those of my fellow homo sapiens, was well-evolved to resist external assault and I was left with a little cut that soon vanished into my growing self.

I left that small lawn on the west side of the Boat Pond and curved my way round its northern end. I slowed and then stopped at the glistening dark bronze statues of Alice in Wonderland with the Mad Hatter and the March Hare dashing around the great mushroom, their coffee-colored soft metal three times life-size caught in a frozen quantum snapshot framed for the children of this world while the immortal beings scamper elsewhere eternally in the multiverse. So familiar yet even more mysterious by night's narrow man-made gleam than they are in the wide and natural rays of day, I paid them a moment's homage as a million children did before me, enjoying the smooth top of the mushroom under my north-pointing palm. I paused for a breath and a questioning gaze at Alice's ringlets, hearing in my forehead the last incomprehensible high-pitched metallic echo of her voice fading out: for I had intruded on the immortals' dispute in their customary privacy of midnight, and knowing they'd resume their actual life as soon as my back was turned, I was off again homewards leaving the great beings in their circle of lamps.

I walked north through the trees behind the benches that bordered the path. The crunching snow carried me safely as I passed the spot where Giana Molise and I had sat literally tripping our brains out (as later events would prove) on a spring afternoon during my senior year in high school. Giana's parents were Italian-from-Italy and she had to be home for dinner, stoned as she was and unthinkable as it seemed to me. At first I thought she was either kidding or wanted to ditch me but she was perfectly serious and so we agreed to meet on the same bench in exactly two hours. I wandered off without her, lonelier than a cloud, for at least a cloud floats comfortably and I alas did not. To pass the time I drifted through the most familiar and familial blocks where I had spent much of my life until that point but little seemed normal—no surprise, for Giana and I had each taken a tab of very potent LSD and anyway my synapses, receptors and the other components of my cranial anatomy had begun to frazzle even before this trip since I was about five weeks into my psychedelic venture.

As I plodded in my daze down the once-homey blocks that now seemed so weird, I felt a growing pressure in the middle of my body that soon centered in my groin. I knew I had to deal with it but I didn't know how because I didn't know what it was—that strange, unfamiliar, really bizarre urge to take a pee. Passing the Lotus, a Chinese restaurant on Third Avenue, I thought, "The Chinese are strangers here too—they can help me." Seeing my stunned seventeen-year old face, the maitre d' at first wanted me out of the restaurant but when I didn't budge he pointed me back towards the bathroom. Yet even there I was unsure what to do until I noticed that the height of the urinal was close to the height of the pressure in my body and gazing down I saw the zipper also at that same meridian and then with some difficulty I undid my fly and put it all together by taking it all out. (After that interlude both ridiculous and sad, Giana and I met at the bench and took the bus down Fifth to see *Yellow Submarine* and for a while the world was perfectly beautiful and vastly entertaining.)

North I walk now through the snow next to the wall untrodden but for tiny bird feet, the bare limbs of the tall shrubs spectral on my left in the stone-shaded gloom, fast as I can towards the gate at 79th street that will send me back into the brighter paved world which brightness I now desire though the concrete holds no appeal— and suddenly, instantly, a great glittering shapeless white shape appears ahead of me on my left, speckled by moonlight and the flanking lamps: Cypress Hill at 79th street, broad and long, a hundred fifty yards of hill from tippiest western top to eastern bottom and wider than long in its many-sloped expanse. How strange and lovely it seemed at first midnight glimpse after a lifetime's friendly acquaintance, so well-known in green by day and the purplish grass of evening, seen now pale surprising folds like a woman's flesh under the moon first given to my view in her mixed shyness and pride. Here I sledded hundreds of times as a child and as a man and here Margie and I had lain together happily one summer night playing with each other's genitals and I with her breasts, utterly remote in our passions in the dark night on these soft acres—until we noticed a tall man running away from us with her pocketbook in his hand, I chased him but he escaped and Margie and I spent half an hour glumly roaming through our fourth-grade playing fields in the back of a police car as the cops stopped one group of black men after another until we'd had enough and I took Margie home.

Not even the snowfields below the Fortress of Quebec, which I saw by full moon from a passing train long after midnight, surpassed in night-time wintry beauty this welcoming childhood slope. So I stopped, I gazed, I breathed, I let my eyes wander up and over the gleaming white and shadowy form illuminated by the three-quarter moon just rising above Fifth Avenue in the east, with a few old lamps along its distant borders. The things of the evening were sufficient unto the evening and not a single thought of Margie rose to my consciousness nor did anything else distract me from the night and the snow curving up vaguely into dim distance and trees, with the scratchy whistles of the wind around my tiring, strong body and the cool air in and out of me.

I just thought it was a great end to a pleasant walk as I pointed north in the snow along the path that was icy smooth as an outdoor rink, towards the gap I could see in the wall at 79th street where I'd soon emerge from this reverie of a crosstown commute. Beginning to feel the gray power of the street ahead and the nature mixed with memories falling contentedly behind me, I looked again at the great white slope indistinct and darkening at its edges and said goodbye in my mind to the spirit of the place. As I walked towards the exit I noticed an odd shape in the shadows on my right next to a small stand of bushes and there on its back with pitted runners pointed at the sky I saw a sled, an actual sled, a wooden skid-alike reproduction of a Flexible Flyer discarded by some famously spoiled child of the upper east side. Dear Reader, know that the sled was there awaiting the moment for which it had been made, and I ran to it incredulous in the night expecting to see it shattered and useless but instead found it lacking only a cotter pin, a tiny piece of metal to hold the steering bar to the metal of the frame. I lifted up its slim, light body, looking around me with a wild surmise as if expecting some onlooker to appear and grab it from me. None came. I felt again the cool night of the park across my shoulders, laid the sled down on the snow and began looking through my pockets for something to replace the cotter pin so I could attempt the hill.

Nothing, nothing and nothing—not in coat, jacket or pants, not the pen nor the pencil nor the credit card sliced into a shred and certainly no twig or stick would hold, so I tossed the sled back into the shrubs and with a barely disappointed smile, for I'd already had a wonderful evening, I started to walk out of the park. Hunching my shoulders a bit, I slid my left hand into my pocket for warmth where my fingers found—my key ring. How my heart did sing for a ring! I hurried back to my wounded comrade, slipped the few keys off the steel ring and into my wallet for safety, kneeled at the broken shoulders of the abandoned wintry warrior and fiddled the flanged metal into the slot where the cotter pin belonged. I twisted it around a few times to make sure it was set and presto—a fine sled I kept for several years, light and fast to skim alone down Cypress Hill in the dimmed dark whiteness!

Quickly a freshened power returned to my body face-first, twinkling from eyes and cheeks down my neck to ripple across my shoulders and drip into my chest where it dissipated into the general electricity of my frame, and the wind flickered with it down the hill from the west south-west to shiver my cheeks, but my eyes were comfortable behind my glasses as I considered the slopes ahead of me. Cypress Hill is really wide, steepest at the center and milder as it sprawls south, darker the higher I looked away from the iron streetlights scattered at its flanks, hiding from the rising moon in the shadow of the trees at the top. And so I began the long climb.

The sled had just a short torn string still attached to

its front steering bar where the spoiled child of luxury had left it, so I had to carry it in one hand and with the moon rising fast in the east above the Hotel Carlyle where President Kennedy rested and played during his many visits to the city and my heart already beating fast, I made my skidding-up way to the uttermost top of the hill. (Despite growing up with an unobstructed view of the eastern horizon across the East River with parents who often showed me the pastel moon rising fat, I never actually understood that like its golden warm brother, the silvery disk also rises in the east and sets in the west; not until I married and fathered and moved to an apartment just north of the city with a full-frontal view of the Hudson river and a bed next to the window, and was awakened one morning at four o'clock by a blistering, glistering huge globe of white silver setting into the dark river, did I grasp that elemental fact.)

I found Cypress Hill much icier and harder to climb than I'd imagined, but I was so excited by the prospect of sledding alone on my favorite hill under the midnight moon that I scampered slipping up the steepest parts instead of working my way woodsman-like zig-zagging against the grain to the top. Cypress Hill's surface is now a manicured pool table after New York's recently terminated run of prosperity with many asphalt trails to scar it and anti-pedestrian fences to protect it, but then it had only the ancient path at the bottom near Fifth that

that had led me north, and only the trees that had been growing since long before I first began to sled it when I was eight, with patchy grass beneath the snow where Margie and I had lain and enjoyed each other's youthful bodies—but as I said, I didn't think of her that evening though I would recollect her the morning after.

When I was about two-thirds up the hill I stopped to look down its glowing curves and I could scarcely believe the beauty and good fortune I'd stumbled into: completely alone in the silent park with just the sound of the quickening wind and the not-quite rhythmic squeezebox of my breath and my purposeful, scrunching steps; the fantastic view of the sweeping-down hill to the east and south, white and dark in the rays and shadows of the iron lamps along the far-bordering paths and the three-quarter moon arching whiter and whiter above the uppermost spire of the Carlyle's cubist tower, all framed by Fifth Avenue's two-hundred foot wall of shaded windows and rich stones. All that and the cool air made my whole face tingle, I forced myself to turn away from the dazzling view before the feeling spread and I climbed towards the darkness uphill between the trees at the peak, trudging where the hill became steepest.

I made my way up to the last extremity where the hill ended in a slim grove of pines next to the northbound Park Drive. I kneeled and put the sled down for my run, holding it tight since the last thing I wanted was to set it free without me. Through a narrow gap in the trees about six feet wide I could see the long ocean of white stretching east where soon I'd be skidding towards the dark shore of Fifth Avenue. The wind had grown stronger from the southwest at my back and now I understood clearly, for I'd had hints before, that a good bit of the excitement I felt was fear: because it's a long hill and it was very icy and despite the lovely glimmerings of the moon on the snow it was quite dark if you actually had to steer; but while I acknowledged my fear I trusted my body, trusted my instincts and I wanted more than anything to have the experience itself.

For a moment like the night I was calm and quiet. Since there was no string to steer with I had to lie belly down flat on the wooden slats of the sled with my one and only face—a pleasant one, and all I've got—just a few inches from the ice. I wasn't thrilled by that but I had sledded just so down this hill many times before, though the older I got the more I liked to sit back and steer with my feet and a strong piece of twine. Yet since my earliest days I have rarely feared committing my body to the earth whether jumping from a high wall into a bed of leaves, playing tackle football with or without equipment, leaping from a bicycle onto the grass in imitation of a fighter pilot ejecting from his jet, or running at sprint speed up a half-broken wooden fence to launch myself into the air after a curving Frisbee; and with only one small broken bone to show for a lifetime of it (not counting two drunken sprains) I had a reasonable confidence in my ability to endure this clattering descent.

In the white gap between the dark young pines, I lay on the sled belly down facing Fifth and briefly reviewed what to expect if I was thrown by one of Newton's laws onto the icy snow: startling, sometimes bruising, occasionally cause for a week or two of limping or a snapped pair of glasses, but nothing worse. Ahhhhh! It was quiet up there in the pines at the top of the hill. I twisted the steering bar with my hands feeling the metal runners make a satisfying scratchy sound as I turned them on the grainy ice. Very nice, I thought—and began to feel myself tumbling into quick-rising whispers of fatigue, no doubt about it, so I took one short breath and started using my hands to paddle the sled downwards, because it was now or never. I began to slide slowly down the gleaming slope that was glistening with promise and the unmistakable reality of fear, and the second pull of my hands on the ground moved the sled irresistibly faster as it was tugged by gravity towards the center of the earth, across the curves of the hill.

As I slid out the white gap in the shadow of the pines, the brightness of the hill struck me instantly, the moonlight and the rim of lamps flickered snowy in my eyelids with a bright glaze that I distinctly felt—or imagined, and there's usually no difference—as the hill's rare pleasure in having me appreciate its beauty in the solitude of the night. My reverie vanished in a quarter of a second replaced by the instinct of self-preservation: because the hill was all about gravity's business big and bright and slick, illumined by the moon and my instant explosion of adrenaline as it swept me faster and faster bumping and sliding, roller-coaster surging fast and faster more skiddingly than I'd ever coursed this snowy hump before.

To live, only time to steer in the white night suddenly noisy with crunching ice and my creaking sled and the whistling wind and the thumping whoosh of my adrenalized heart. Not quite swallowing my first cool gulp of speeding dread as I bounced over the ice, time itself moving both too fast and strangely slow, I twisted the steering bar away from the steep center of the hill that seemed ready to smash me, shuddering towards the right where I thought I could more easily endure. On the gritty ice the sled skidded like a car turning too tight, the left runner clattering off and on the ice with the wind and my brain whooshing and whistling but I kept running to the right where the slope was gentler, no time to scan ahead for the best way as I launched over a Buick-sized bump into the air and landed with a ball-bouncing, stomach-shaking shudder at full speed, had a split second of smoothness then bubbled over a little Volkswagen-sized hump, shimmied fast down a gentle hillock and found myself suddenly with the body of Cypress Hill behind me to the north!!

Safe, as I streaked towards an iced asphalt path, not the one I'd traveled north beside but another smooth way leading south. I felt a smile shape my face as I made the path coasting quick with all the momentum that had carried me scarily down, the runners now gliding with a quiet slick, relief and happiness flowing across my body with the wind, the sparse elms and maples standing aside respectfully in the night, blurry at first and then more distinct as I relaxed in the embrace of the irresistible forces pulling me yet towards the center of earth and south through Central Park. Delight at the shapes of landscape sliding behind me, pleasure having pushed aside fear with the adrenaline remaining because—I had made it! I hadn't hurt myself and I was having by far the greatest ride of my life in this night of surprise after surprise, full of pure joy at the moment.

I felt the cold air across my face like the most refreshing ocean wave of summer with the taste of springtime too in the fresh dirt damp smell of the icy grit that I churned as I glided down the icy path from 78th to 77th to 76th to 75th street, slower and slower in a calm capitulation of slope to resistance until I had to reach down and use my hands again pulling myself along the icy way, but then the path became steeper and icier flanked by a higher slope that must have poured more water during its runny warm hours of the afternoon and I began to move more easily again between manual assists, enjoying the work part of it now, something different after the pure motion of hurtling downhill. I found myself approaching the Boat Pond where I'd started and saw a short path that would lead me back to the great bronze statues of Alice and her friends, so I leaned hard into my work as if paddling a small boat on a calm sea and I emerged into the brightly lit circle around the shining great statues.

Generations of children and famously Jimi Hendrix had sat on the mushroom, hugged the white rabbit and otherwise enjoyed this sublime manifestation of a perfect fantasy. The beautiful imagined beings glowed with an undeniable reality in the electric light of March's midnight and I felt them again caught in motion, frozen for my mortal eyes with their high-pitched incomprehensible conversation quick-stopped beyond my fleshy ears. Nor were they welcoming as usual for this was their private time and I had disturbed them twice this evening, so I calmly paddled my cold hands on the sparse ice, barely looking up at their mysterious beauty. I slid myself to the two short steps that led down to the Sailboat Pond where this circular journey had originated, pushed myself in fast clunks down and with a final surge of inertia I came to rest facing south across the empty concrete basin. Sledding in a single midnight moonlit swoop from Cypress Hill to Alice in Wonderland and the Boat Pond—thank you very much, I respectfully told the universe.

I took one short look at the congratulatory lights around the concrete oval and struggled to my feet, turned towards Alice with the sled under my arm and set my feet moving north again, wordlessly happy in my tired but so-satisfied body. I was moving on instinct now, my body feeling light after the adrenaline rush, the wind whistling a little louder in my ears, the park seeming darker too. And in fact this path was darker with fewer lamps, taller trees and so close to Fifth that the moon was blocked but I was good at swallowing my trepidation and making my way in the darkness—a most human skill that has served me both well and poorly—and I emerged soon enough in the reflected lunar glow at the foot of Cypress Hill, the sled under my arm again, the hill still silent and slick and yet more welcoming, the moon having risen just that much higher over the Hotel Carlyle's modernist tower, yet more light and yet more white.

How fabulous it would be to go again! I thought, and took a few steps up the slope but wisdom, helped by a cold whistling wind, quite literally stopped me in my tracks as it so rarely does and I thought: I can never improve on that ride and I could easily fall off and get hurt now that I'm more tired, I'll quit while I'm ahead. And though quitting while ahead wasn't a strategy I often applied except for my policy of leaving bars while a favorite song still played on the jukebox, this time I tucked the sled under my arm and walked out of the park at 79th and Fifth into the right-angled concrete world of humans and machines, across the street from the Metropolitan Museum and catty-corner from the apartment building where Reggie Jackson used to live and my friend Jacob Weinberg's mom bought an apartment after she sold the Scarsdale house, though Jake never lived there because he hung himself in his basement three days before his freshman year would have started at Harvard. (Close friend and doubly-doomed child of sadness, Jake is # 014-293137 in the Death File and is buried about twenty yards from where my own dear father came to rest almost thirty years later on a peaceful field between low ridges, just twelve minutes up the hill from where I live.)

I don't remember whether I took a cab or bus the twelve blocks from 79th street homeward but soon enough I entered the welcoming darkness of my neighborhood pub with the sled still under my arm. I grabbed a stool near the front of the bar between the only two customers, an attractive young woman with long legs and big feet pointing out of a long maroon skirt, and a red-faced old man asleep with his head in his arms on the bar next to a large glass of Irish whiskey and a bowl of chili. I had never seen the woman before—her name, I would learn, was Anna Seeley—but the man was John Curley, who worked around the corner as a union doorman from four to midnight and usually had his late supper here. John remembered sitting on his father's shoulders in a vast crowd on Fifth Avenue as Teddy Roosevelt waved from the back of an open Cadillac in the 1914 presidential campaign and he had a perfect knowledge of American history, the long sequence he had lived through as well the portion that preceded it, along with one of the best collections of Indian and Central Asian coins in the United States.

The bar, called Puddings and now long-gone, was dim and still with the smell of slightly stale beer and old french fries, its dark stained plywood setting the quiet tone. I rested my sled against the base of the bar, pulled in my chair, smiled Hi at the woman who smiled politely back, and waved to the bartender who was fifteen feet away near the kitchen washing glasses. I pulled in my stool with a slight grinding sound that woke John. He stirred his head up, blinked his eyes open, looked around, saw me and instantly said,

"Khiva the golden! Jewel of the Oxus! Flower of Khorasan!"

Anna was startled—I guessed this was the first she'd seen John awake and thought he was just a crazed old drunk—but I answered back in my best Persian to recite a poem of Omar Khayyam, "Yek qatriye ahb, bah dariashad; yek dariye khak, ba zamin yektashad..." and finished the verse with Omar's two lines following, modern as the English of Yeats or Eliot though written nine hundred years before them: There was a drop of water that went away with the sea, a speck of dirt that became one with the earth.... John shook his head in affirmation, laughed and slapped the bar.

"Good boy, Bobby, good boy—a beer for my friend Bobby!"

The sad-eyed, kind-hearted dried-out drunk artist-biker bartender moved towards the tap and when John saw Anna laughing with us he said,

"And another drink for the young lady please."

Of course when the beer arrived I had to recite a little more Omar, he who sang so well of the cup and its contents and soon John, Anna and I were all laughing together and sharing tales of distant lands and times, for Anna had a masters in Byzantine art history and had worked for two years at the Boston Museum of Fine Arts; John's sixty years of coin collecting had given him a literally encyclopedic knowledge of European, Middle Eastern and Central Asian history and iconography; and I, dabbler of the trio, had studied with the world's greatest authority on Central Asian languages, the Altaic philologist Karl Menges, while I took courses with other teachers in old, middle and modern Iranian.

Anna's eyes were deep-set and large, big and circular

at the center and tapering to slim, long Egyptian-seeming settings that stretched to the edge of her temples. Her cheekbones were flat and long and triangular, wide at the top and pointing down her chin and her forehead was flat too, her face cubist and very pretty, reddish-brown hair in a quick, short cut across the chiseled plane of her forehead. She listened intently as John told us he had that day taken delivery of two Sogdian coins from about 700AD, each about the size of a silver dollar, gold with Indian script on them—the Sogdians were deep into their Buddhist phase just before the final onslaught of Islam—and she listened in turn to me as I refreshed John's summary knowledge of the Sogdians: speakers of an east Iranian language probably related to Scythian and perhaps more distantly to Ossetian, they were the first inhabitants of Samarkand and Roxanne who married Alexander the Great was a daughter of the Sogdian king; they spread widely across Central Asia but were wiped out completely by the Mongol invasions and those who survived were absorbed by the larger Persian-speaking population.

"Here's to the Sogdians, the Tocharians and the Kwarezmians! Noosh!" John said—drink, in the language of Omar, and he hoisted his dripping glass of Irish whiskey.

"Noosh!" I replied.

"Slante!" said Anna, showing the easily-imagined

Celtic origins of her beauty as we toasted those inhabitants of the distant oases, Zoroastrians and Buddhists, fire-worshippers and Moslems, melon growers and weavers, gazers at the sky. Then I did my imitation of the first day of Professor Menges' seminar on Middle Eastern Languages and Cultures when with a forehead as deeply indented as Dick Tracy's enemy Prune-Face, he spoke in a comically thick German accent of "Hither und thither Asia" which I understood only later was an English expression for the near and far east. John could barely maintain his balance as he laughed, spitting out "Hither und thither Asia" over and over again as his red face got really bright and he slurped down the rest of his glass in coughing little swallows.

Then it was Anna's turn. Her thin lips easily held our attention with a story about the small museum outside of Boston where she once worked and the old Irish janitor who was ordered to burn an excess mummy, a bundle of ancient linen barely four feet long wrapped around twenty pounds of unidentified remains. A young curator clearing forgotten artifacts brought him the mummy to use as fuel during a cold winter, but the janitor would not burn it because he was a believer in the Christian sacrament of burial even for ancient infidels, and for fear of breaking the contemporary law for improper disposal of a corpse. He was, however, willing to take the curator to the basement and stand by as the young man opened the heavy iron door of the coal furnace and tossed the mummy in. Before the curator could even shut the door, said the janitor with a thick brogue in Anna's vivacious imitation,

"That poor old Egyptian flared up like biggest Fourth of July you ever saw and didn't he burn the eyebrows off the curator and scare the living bejesus out of me, I don't mind telling you."

John could barely maintain his balance as he laughed and laughed and his reddish face grew truly crimson but despite the artfulness of Anna's rendition the unlikely drama might well be true, because all museums are always short of space, there are many more mummies in the world than you think, and most of them do burn wildly since they're often preserved with asphalt-like extracts and saltpeter, a chemical that was later used to make gunpowder. When he recovered his breath from his laughing jag, John excused himself to struggle off the bar stool and waddle to the bathroom. Anna drained her drink, began to put on her coat and looked at me through her wide, now undeniably Egyptian-seeming eyes that had darkened with the hour. She said matter-of-factly in a quiet, unsmiling voice,

"Do you think you could take me home?" I was surprised though it had already been a surprising night, but I was careful to match her down-to-earth mood with my own and merely said, "Sure, I'd be glad to." I reached down to pick up my sled and I guess she hadn't noticed it because she said,

"What are you doing with that?"

"I was walking home through Central Park and I found it, I guess some kid left it there, it was a little broken but I fixed it with my key ring and actually I had a really good ride, I guess I might as well keep it."

"Interesting," she said and looked away. There was a large suitcase tucked into the corner beside her, she reached for it but I said, "Let me take that."

"Thanks." She finished putting on her coat, I made sure there was enough money on the bar and followed her into the street. John was still in the bathroom as we left—he often spent a while there and you didn't want to be the next man in—and once we were out in the cold, refreshing night on narrow old Lexington I told her,

"You know, I live literally right around the corner if you'd like to come up."

"OK, fine," and now she relaxed and smiled a bit as I took the heavy suitcase and hauled it just around the corner onto my block. She carried my sled and we walked quietly as her eyes took in the handsome midnight street, the rich-looking old buildings with great windows and shining tall doors on the north side where the millionaires lived, the massive brick church at the end of the block across Park Avenue pushing its wide walls out to the corner, the leafless elm trees disappearing into the street lights' glare.

She seemed about to say something but then she leaned over and gave me a little peck on the lips, but the best part was her half-closed eyes, wide and shapely mysterious like the wealthy women of Roman Egypt still vivid on their wooden tombstones back at the museum, and her lovely secret smile when she turned away and her cheeks formed small, perfectly rounded pinkish pillows high on her angular cheekbones under her wide eyes, a beautiful sight that made me very happy. She reached out and took my hand and while I'd noticed that her hands like her feet were large, now I could feel the cool strength of them. She lifted my hand up to her lips and gave it a warm, moist kiss and for the first time I felt my body begin to quicken, by which I mean my balls started to tingle and my penis to grow. We walked in silence for half a minute and soon ascended the three steep, steep flights up to my apartment. She looked around— it was a nice place with a good-sized living-room and tiled fireplace, high ceilings, old wooden shutters, many bookshelves in the living rooms and lining the walls of what had once been a dining room, and a narrow hallway stretching just out of sight.

"You have a lot of books," she said in her slightly grainy, tired voice

"This is true." She took off her coat, draped it over a straight-backed wooden chair, walked over to the gray tweed couch and let her long body drop into a corner.

"Do you have anything to smoke?" Her voice had a touch of the midwest— I would learn she was from Syracuse—and she gazed calmly around my apartment which was a bit cluttered and messy. Though I didn't keep it that way for any reason other than habit and always cleaned up as well as I could when expecting company, I had learned that women liked it that way: surrounded as they were by so many uptight New Yorkers, they saw my environment as proof of the friendly soul they'd been attracted to while its walls of books, interspersed with antique maps of Iran and Cagney posters and Durer prints and framed science fiction magazines, was evidence of other aspects of my nature they might enjoy. I'd smoked a bit of a joint before I went to the museum and I found half of it on top of an empty beer can. I lit the match for her as she smoked a few deep breaths then she took my wrist and pulled me next to her on the couch, put her lips over mine and breathed her smoke into me. She grabbed through my pants at my lumpy dick, pressing and kneading it as she pushed her face into my neck and drove her tongue under my ear. Instant action, clumsy but well meant!

I stroked her long, silky cheeks with my fingers, delighting in their incredible softness, let my hand move down her neck under her short-cut hair, felt the hot pulse in her throat, moved my face to kiss her taught skin stretched between straining tendons that smelled faintly of perfume. She was jamming her hand under my shirt, rubbing my hairy chest and squeezing the muscles around a nipple as I put my hand over the smooth hair at the top of her head, tilted it to the side and kissed at her cheek, hoping to make that fine little round flower bloom again at the top of her cheek.

"You don't have to kiss me," she said in that grainy hint-of-the-heartland voice.

I moved my face back just a bit and looked at her huge, cloudy eyes.

"But I like kissing you, I find it very pleasant. Your skin is so smooth and soft, it's really unlike mine"—I took her hand and brushed its back against my cheek with its two-day beard—

"and your eyes are so beautiful, so large and deeply set and look how far they run all the way under your handsome forehead, I hope you don't mind part of you being called handsome instead of the more traditional female adjectives."

I stroked the wide expanse above her eyes; she laughed, pulled my face up to hers, stuck her tongue down my throat and reached down with both hands to unbuckle my pants and grabbed my now fully-compliant pointer, stiff and fat and striving. While holding it with one hand she pulled up her skirt and yanked at her underpants and as I helped pull them down, she unbuttoned her blouse and pulled her bra down to expose her smallish right tit.

I guess it had been a long day for her and she was a young woman in a hurry. Her thighs were long and smooth and very attractive to me just then as she wiggled her ass back on the sofa, moving her knees up a bit as she tugged me forward to her monumental, breathtaking, light-brown furry cleft that seemed to stretch most of a foot from its vague beginnings down near her butt, up and up in a widening V towards her belly button. Even at this late hour I would have preferred to spend some timeless but considerable time touching her naked female curves and flats and silks and furs, globes and crevices large and small, damp and dry on the bed in the bedroom that was just a few feet away—and having her touch my own muscled and rewarding body, soothing and pleasing me before we joined at the hips—but my new friend had her own urgent agenda, one to which I reflexively agreed with an emphatic, cylindrical, reddish and straining-upwards one-eyed gesture. So I moved closer and reached down to her pussy to find it already running wet, wet on top and wet inside and wet all around what I instantly felt was an interior vastness, and my touching made her even more urgent with desire and she pulled me suddenly into her and jutted towards me with a great sigh of relief that I felt hot and damp on my face.

I was in, and she put her arms around my neck and pulled me tight as I worked forward and back and side to side on my feet and onto my knees into and all around her steaming great interior, reaching out with one hand to caress the tit she'd exposed, kissing her pretty face and pressing my lips against her magnificent closed eyes that were straining round under the lids, then putting the tip of my tongue at one large ear which seemed to make her uncomfortable so I stopped, but then she pulled my lips over to hers again and for the first time opened her mouth to me instead of skidding her large tongue into mine, and three seconds after my tongue had joined the rest of me enjoying the moistness inside of her she started to moan and twitch and her pussy went into spasms and she pulled her mouth away from mine and put her hands under her ass and bobbed her butt and made whining, panting baby noises and then suddenly drenched me in a stream, an absolute river of juice as she clutched at me inside and out.

Was it a minute or maybe three I'd been inside her? Not I the great lover but she the impassioned one desperately needing what she'd chosen, and when her fine, strong body had stopped its shivering and a sleepy peace drained the tension from her skin and muscles, she kissed my face once tenderly and then relaxed as I resumed my jamming, taking a moment to stroke at her long, smooth thighs, to reach under the top of the great mound for her impressive clitoris, easily dragging a thumbful of her own liquid to smooth the hidden spheroid, scrunching between my knuckles the springy mound where it was hidden. Now I pulled down the other half of her bra so both tits were bouncing and easily kissed as I worked hard to find the sides of her great pussy and more easily the top, but in her satisfaction her face and her neck and her hair had become all the more open to me in the sweep of her collarbone down to her breasts and finally I reached under her waist with one hand and under her neck with the other and slid her down onto her back on the grainy old sofa so I could get at her whole lovely face and neck and breasts with my face, to grab under her ass and pull her close to me as I reached inside and pushed and grinded away for joy, and when she put her hand around my neck and pulled my face to hers and just wiggled the tip of her tongue into my mouth—that was it, that rare delicacy drew me out and up and in and over her, draining happily into her truly great valley.

I lay beside her for a moment then extricated myself as she rolled over on the couch and started to go to sleep but I told her, "I have a nice bed just in there," and I pointed through the louvered door that had been half-open the whole time. "Now you tell me," she said with a smile and walked into the dark room, three-quarters filled by my double bed where she lay down, pulled a crumpled sheet and blanket over her and went right to sleep. I thought for a second about laying down next to her but I was thirsty so I walked out through the living room and down the hall to the bathroom, ran the water cold in the sink and washed my face and the back of my neck, cupped my hands and drank deep from New York's delicious well. Refreshed, I came to bed and lay down next to my new friend's long and delicious frame. She seemed asleep but as I lay next to her gazing in the soft gloom at the wide, stretched ovals of her sleeping eyes, stroking gently the flat pillows of her long buttocks—she suddenly pulled me close, wiggling her hips against mine and I felt her entirely alive and near me, embracing the closeness of my body for itself and not merely for her own release. I felt our magnetisms truly interpenetrating in a slow, moist, multi-limbed entwining that left me tingling and warm and deeply satisfied from the top of my head down to my toes, front to back and everywhere in between, joyfully losing myself into her hips and the smooth, strong flesh of her high-timbered neck.

We both slept well and I awoke with Anna's hand on my cock on and her tongue on my face. Excusing myself to piss away the night's effluvia, I returned and perhaps for the sake of completeness, she quickly kissed her way down my body and helped herself to a heaping mouthful of me. I pulled away the sheets so I could see the pretty sight she made in the filtered, indistinct northern light that came through my rice-paper blinds, her wide triangular cheekbones moving up and down over my cock and I reached over to get a few fingers in her pussy, marveling again at its capacity and its dampness, a virtual stream instantly flowing. When she started to take my balls in her mouth, that was a little more attention than I wanted just then so I pulled her head towards me and she climbed onto me, carefully moving her tits around my face as her needs and mine required. I came first and quickly in a dizzying surge and then with fast-fumbling fingers and the remainder of my erection, I brought her to a spasmodic peace in a crazed gusher of she-juice. She went instantly to shower, changed into clean clothes from the large suitcase she had with her, gave me a chaste kiss on the cheek, and lugged her bag down the stairs off to work.

Although I called her four or five times after that, I never saw Anna again but for one short meeting in a restaurant where she had iced tea and I had iced coffee. She said she'd really enjoyed the sex and thought I was a nice guy and very smart, but she had a boyfriend she was in love with, and the night we met she was coming home from a visit with him that had ended in a fight, and she hoped I'd understand. I told her the truth: I understood perfectly and though I would very much like to see her again—long-legged Egyptian-eyed art historians with midnight hot pants being high on my list of life's great joys—all she needed was to tell me just once that she didn't want to go out with me, and I would have stopped calling. Her eyes grew kind and almost sad when I told her that, and we parted on friendly terms.

That morning after Anna left my apartment, I got in the bath for a soak. The tub was almost six feet long with no overflow drain so you could really take the water cure. As the tub filled, first tickling then encasing my balls in a kind fluidic tingle and lifting up my triangular flotation unit in a warm embrace, I began to recall the new secretarial assistant on the 39th floor, nineteen and muddy red-haired, and I confess that one of my hands— recto or verso, I will not state— reached down to keep my white whale's breathing hole above the water, the pale apparition growing stronger with every passing second as I met Jeanie in the elevator bank and she was wearing her fluffy white sweater over her schoolgirl's button-down blue shirt, and her breasts filled out the top so nicely wide and full under the waves of hair red in the sunlight through the dusty window across her strong athletic shoulders, and she smiled as we walked down the deserted hallway under construction on 41 where the firm hadn't yet filled in the empty offices, and we found one, I shut the door behind us and she smiled and took my hand and I reached over to turn her face to me and kissed her, those big pink lips and we kissed and she laughed and then we were sitting together on the floor and she had her skirt up and her pants down and her knees wide and her hand on my cock and I was on my knees and popped out a large, sweet breast and then I was into and into and into her—and, and, and, and then I must have napped briefly in the bath because I remember waking with the water near my nose: and startled I arose, showered hot then briefly cold, quarried in the closet for something less gamy than yesterday's underwear and triumphantly discovered the remains of a bag of clean stuff.

That was good! Quickly into shirt and tie—when you wear the male uniform from seventh grade through twelfth, you never lose your instant facility with a knot— then pants and finally, hopelessly, searching for socks and settling for a close but imperfect match, not quite actually clean. Then a breather to open wide the blinds, dark-stained pine over the great windows as the soft northern light streams in, and finding the remains of last night's joint on top of a beer can, quickly vaporizing that in two little pulls, then seeing the marvelous cardboard square of The Who's My Generation leaning against the corner, four slim youths with Big Ben behind them no louder than they, and slipping that onto my turntable with the first twanging beauty notes of "The Good's Gone"—and indeed it was, or as much of it remained to me that morning, because I decided to poke around in the lacquered pine dresser for a small baggie wherein I found one M & M-sized gold and red bud of premium Jamaican marijuana, smelling like cocoanut mixed with cloves. I crunched and rolled and burned its fragrance while turning up The Who as a sort of caffeine, feeling the smoke in my lungs and my eyes and my ears and my head, and then all was light and happy—for a minute or ten, anyway.

****

Up until this moment the previous twelve hours had been more or less appropriate for an enthusiastic unmarried twenty-five year old male. If it was an unusual pleasure to escort a young woman home when I knew her insane love for John Lennon would thwart any actual romance of mine, I can scarcely be blamed for my curiosity and perhaps applauded for my kindness. Sledding down the icy white peak of Central Park at midnight to the foot of Alice in Wonderland in a spoiled rich kid's abandoned sled was wonderful by any standard, and I continue to believe that the religious of many denominations would accept my pleasures with the lovely art historian given that we were both unmarried, over twenty-one, and no lies were told. Re the legal drug, alcohol, that's killed fifty million Americans in my lifetime and the illegal herb by moonlight that's never killed anyone: well, this world of death and taxes is often too much with us and I, like many taxpayers, find the occasional escape to be highly therapeutic.

As for touching the glory of my manhood in the bath, writers far more saintly than I have attested that these things do happen. But only a fool such as I was then, and remained for a quite a while afterwards, could imagine that smoking strong pot before going to work in the morning was anything other than a really bad idea, and worse in practice.

I won't try to describe what I thought or felt after the sweet electric sound of The Who faded from the speakers and I went out the door. I don't remember specifically, but I was certainly in a short-lived brain-buzzing ignorant euphoria as I descended the steep stairs to the clean sidewalks of my brownstone block, heading to Fifth Avenue for the bus that would take me to Rockefeller Center and my office on the 41st floor of the RCA Building. I remember it was a nice morning when I could smell the sweet dampness of imminent spring in the air; though I can still visualize the walk two blocks west to Fifth Avenue, because I took that same route for more than ten years, I don't recall anything that happened until I was seated on the M4 bus approaching 80th street where the Museum ends, I looked to my right and there was Cypress Hill where I'd sledded last night, now scarred with streaks of black dirt in the warming sunlight.

I know I was sitting in the back of the crowded bus near the rear right window, and I know that my mind was a jumble from the reefer and everything else, and I know there was a muttering, mentally ill woman in tattered clothes near me, and I also know that I thought about Margie for the first time as we crossed 79th street to the bus stop, remembering the night we were lying on the hill then green with summer and her purse was stolen as we played grown-up games with each other's young bodies.

All this I know for fact: and also that as soon I began to think about Margie, the disturbed woman started to moan and chatter louder, and between the jagged interior crashing of my brainwaves and the loud lurching noises of the bus and her rising voice, I became convinced that she was talking about Margie and me in the first person as if she was Margie, first ranting about the night we'd lain on the hill and then about that time when I put on my mother's clothes because Margie wanted me to seduce a female friend of hers cross-dressed as the prelude to a threesome. (I looked pretty good except for my hair but lacking either a wig or a ladylike hat with veil, I refused to take the elevator downstairs past the doorman who'd known me since I was eight, despite Margie's pleas and her friend's promised compliance and the bottle of disgusting Boone's Farm Apple Wine I'd consumed.)

There in the crowd of east side commuters riding down Fifth Avenue to their midtown offices, I heard the woman twitching and muttering louder what seemed to be my dead lover's memories. I tried to ignore her but I couldn't as my shoulders tightened, my breath grew shallow, my forehead and my left eye started to throb and a chilling fear began to rise from the pit of my stomach up through my body to meet the raging discomfort in my head. Tortured by the voice in the bus I chose to flee rather than fight my emotions, so I lurched to my feet as we pulled into 76th street, moving in rhythm to the crescendo of brakes and with a few excuse me's to clear my path, I slapped open the back doors and ran onto the sidewalk, then took off walking as fast as possible fifteen yards to the park's entrance.

Once I'd left the street and had the park's landscape around me I stopped to take a few long, long breaths, trying to shake the freakiness from my eyes and my head—but I couldn't, so I breathed deeply again and began to walk slowly the mile or so to my office south through Central Park in the gauzy morning light. Though the paths had been ice underfoot just ten hours ago this morning was more spring than winter, the damp earth smell was everywhere with the sharp chirping of sparrows, the cool humidity now uncomfortable in my lungs after the warm smoke I'd inhaled, and I worried about my shoes, and puddles, and poodles pissing against the bare trees that looked dying and gray by sunlight.

As I walked I told myself the obvious truth: of course the woman hadn't been reciting Margie's narrative about our vanished nights, I was merely projecting my deeply stoned thoughts onto the surface of her guttural monologue which was a perfectly normal and reasonable thing (as it were) when you were stoned as I was. Unfortunately the problem with my nervous system was not immediately amenable to reason and I was still half-terrified after a few moments walk through the melting soot-smeared ice. Trying to find some calm in the rush hour, I found a new approach: if the sad woman on the bus had been telling Margie's story—and it was just barely possible though supremely unlikely—it was my brain activity in this world she'd been registering since the alpha-, beta-, delta-waves of my thoughts, like everybody else's, were an electromagnetic fact that indeed had been well-tested in my father's office on the digital electroencephalograph that he and his partner had patented.

Giving myself this new hypothesis seemed to help, though probably it was just the walking and breathing, but still I was spooked as I reversed the path of last night's glory in today's muddy yet too-bright morning, seeking dry asphalt. Never before, at least not since my first two or three months on the job, had I been so eager to get to the office. I longed to enter the huge, soothing, sleek marble lobby of the RCA Building for the non-stop ride to 41 in the cherry wood elevator, to reach the big, silent men's room where I could cool my face with running water and empty my bowels in the privacy of my favorite stall, and then to my computer room looking south across midtown at the majestic sharp lines of the Empire State Building and the distant Trade towers tiny behind it, perhaps taking a well-deserved break to fortify myself with an egg sandwich and iced coffee before resuming my struggle to make our nation safe from the depredations of the Great International Uranium Cartel.

I soaked the leather soles of my shoes and wetted my toes in the freezing melt as I worked my way south to my sanctuary. It was work indeed to carry the stone of my hungover fear, choosing paths I hadn't walked the night before—ten hours ago that seemed like ten months—until the first press of fearful energy faded and I sat for a moment on a bench to rest beside the Rowboat lake. How bright had been the wintry night and how dread weird the springing day though its sunny quickening would normally have filled me, earth-bound creature that I am, with intimations of green and future happiness. Still, I began to feel the worst of my stoned desperation melting away to leave me merely anxious and profoundly uncomfortable.

I sat on the bench overlooking the lake where the wooden shells of boats lay belly down against the sky. Empty like them, I was hoping for a redemptive vision and I started to think about making an offering to Margie's imaginary ghost, to bring something fresh and sweet of her into my consciousness as a way of saying goodbye. Just then I pressed my hands into my jacket pockets to warm them and I encountered a crinkly forgotten package of crackers from some soupy snack. I took out the package and reflexively tore it open but before I got the crackers to my mouth I saw a scab on top of my index finger, a minor wound from a battle with a stubborn staple that hadn't wanted to be removed—and I suddenly smiled, for now I could offer something tasty to Margie's hypothetical spirit and bring this interlude to an end.

According to the most ancient and well-respected sources, the spirits of the dead crave a taste of damp blood and are soothed by a sprinkling of pure white flour. It's been well-documented to have worked for Odysseus, so why not now for me? I quickly climbed up the mossy mini-cliff of New York schist overlooking the lake and found a clean and natural-seeming spot to make my sacrifice. I crushed the crackers between my palms into a lumpy powder, scattered the white stuff on the ground, scratched off the scab on my finger with my pinky nail. I squatted above the clean white flour and squeezed painfully hard on my finger until one drop of lovely dark red lifeblood emerged, and kept squeezing until it dropped onto the bleached crumbs. Then I smiled and felt the smile spreading over my face—and being able to amuse myself is a gift that I haven't lost yet, thankfully.

Assuming that I had thus called poor Margie's spirit closer though gratefully feeling none of it, I closed my eyes for a moment, tried with some success to feel peaceful and suddenly began to recall a mild summer night when Margie and I walked to Carl Schurz Park on East End Avenue across the street from where I grew up. We climbed down from the broad walk above the East River to a tiny, hidden patch of grass on a stone pedestal just ten feet over the water, next to Gracie Mansion where the mayor lives. Screened by a tree against the wall from the occasional pedestrians on the walkway above our heads, we sat in our hidden garden looking out across the roiling big flat of water called Hell's Gate where the East River meets the Long Island Sound, with the lights of Randall's Island, Manhattan State Hospital and the Triborough Bridge twinkling in the humid night.

We could smell the salt in the warm darkness as the high tide bubbled north, and we leaned against each other and talked about the summer camps we'd gone to, tennis and hikes and weird kids and dances, and much about the various lakes where we'd swum as children, we both liked those cool green escapes. My stories made her laugh more than I'd ever seen before, it was so nice to see the sharp light in her pale gray eyes and her pretty smile, and after a while she kissed me lightly on the lips, unbuttoned her shirt a bit and placed my hands on her breasts, put her arms around my neck and kissed me again as if she really cared, then we undid each other's pants and she crawled onto me, sitting in my lap with her arms and legs around me, leaning back against the strength of my arms with the river rolling in high tide from the sea below us.

We held each other like that for a long time and I never felt Margie so relaxed and passionate and close. I stayed inside her after I came the first time and I don't think I'd yet smelled anything as delicious as the mix of her own fresh lightly-scented body with the rare sweet salt smell of the river and the mossy green arising from our little island of ferns and grass. We spent two or three hours there as evening turned to midnight, talking and having sex, maybe even making love, then we climbed up over the fence onto the path to startle an older couple walking a small dog, and we finally shared a black and white ice cream soda at the diner on York Avenue where I put her in a cab to take her home to 72nd street.

With the light of the yellow cab shrinking down the street in my mind, Margie was gone to peace at last and I temporarily convinced myself that I was feeling much better. Left only with a headache, tight forehead, aching eyes, wet shoes, rising body odor, a queasy full stomach and too-sensitive ears, I scampered down hopefully from the huge boulder and crossed the great brick playground of Bethesda Fountain, empty on a workday morning but once the northern outdoor capital of hippie New York as Washington Square was the southern.

The sound of the taxis cutting through the park drifted down the monumental staircases to the big empty plaza, but as much time as I'd spent there since I was four, my jangled head remained blissfully silent but for a quick remembrance of the field where we'd played the dying game, just over the hill to the right. Still pointing south to my office, I walked between the two vast and curving late Victorian staircases through a great arched hallway to the central staircase, forty feet wide granite steps gray up into the morning light. And halfway up on the right my destination, the Men's Room where an open door promised relief.

While under different circumstances I might have chosen to sit for a moment, it didn't seem like a good idea just then in Central Park so I looked around for a urinal, unfamiliar with the layout since the place had just reopened after having been closed for years. Two dozen ancient high ivory receptacles lined both sides of a long room and at the far end stood the sole patron, a tall, husky broad-shouldered man with graying hair. He turned to check me out briefly with a neutral expression as anyone might—was I an ax murderer or merely a pisser?—and then he stepped away from the wall, lit by the grimy window above his head, to display in a casual one-handed grip what I first thought was a child's toy baseball bat he carried to warn away muggers. As he raised his eyebrows high and smiled quizzically at me, I realized it was meat and not maple in his hands and he was showing me his gargantuan member as an invitation to partake.

Suddenly the room's archaic porcelain lost its charm and my sense of urgency leapt from groin to head. Leaving the smiling behemoth to future admirers in his marble cave, I reversed field out the door and carried my water into the light of morning. Relieved to be alone again under the brightening sun, I walked up the broad stairs that pointed due south towards the RCA Building, snickering at this most mortal of apparitions as I hurried past the Bandshell, pleased to be back again in this world, tacky though it sometimes was. I gazed at the big curved structure where I'd tried to sing last night and saw only dingy concrete surrounded by patchy-skinned trees. Pleased with their mundane appearance and concerned with nothing more than avoiding the puddles, I gathered speed under the great avenue of elms, pledged to myself that from this moment I would enter the workday much more tranquilly than I began it, and soon was advancing down Fifth Avenue through the morning throngs under the brightening sky, smiling at both my own foolishness and the rising humid freshness of the morning air.

A few minutes later I reached the Rockefellers' most glorious ziggurat, sleek with marble and steel and brass, grateful to be part of it and just fifteen minutes late. Ascending in the perfect cherry wood elevator nonstop to the 41st floor, I hurried into the immaculate men's room, emerged clean and fresh and happy, walked down a flight of stairs to the firm's cafeteria where I got an egg sandwich and iced coffee, and scooted back up to my own small office with its one wide window on Manhattan in the morning stretched north to the horizon. The muddy-white rectangle of Central Park seemed blissfully distant; I sipped my coffee, opened my files and gratefully reentered the clean, logical world of the international uranium cartel.

███

Robbie Saltaire

About the author

Robbie Saltaire was born and grew up in Manhattan. He's worked as house-painter, editor, teacher and as a server at the fabled Papaya King. He currently lives a few miles north of his native Manhattan. You can find him at *robbiesaltaire.com*

9 781887 276979